salmonpoetry

Diverse Voices from Ireland and the World

MORE PRAISE FOR DAVID McLOGHLIN

In a number of breathlessly long sentences, this poem locates within the drama of Antarctic adventure an Irish singer-adventurer who sings the old way, that is, alone. The diction here is as rough as the unforgiving icy environment, and the physical exertion of singing plus the power of his song adds up to its own heroic achievement.

—BILLY COLLINS
Judge's citation on the poem "Tom Crean Sings Sean-Nós at the Tiller on the Southern Ocean" (included), prize-winning finalist in the 2015/2016 Ballymaloe International Poetry Prize

David McLoghlin's debut collection, Waiting for Saint Brendan and Other Poems, *proves strong on first reading and grows richer... with each subsequent rereading. ... The poems are rhetorically baroque, inward-looking, and taut with imagery, and his complex metaphors unfold, slow and origami-like, often across multiple stanzas. ...This is a necessary book, one well worth reading and returning to.*

—ERIC BLIMAN
Birmingham Poetry Review, Spring 2014, number 41

Santiago Sketches *is a gift-box brimming with luminous local details of a loved place through which—over a space of nine months—the poet moves like a pilgrim of the senses, offering in poem after poem what's been seen, felt, smelled, heard; what's been touched, tasted, and understood: Flap of a pigeon's wing ... A dark-eyed girl in purple slippers . . . an angel raises a star/ among the horses . . . At the fountain, the junkies/ washing their needles. What McLoghlin has composed in this adventurous new collection is a scrupulously tolerant anatomy of Santiago, a religious, secular, open-eyed, warts-and-all love letter to a city where he—a stranger—managed for a little, unforgettable while to make himself at home.*

—EAMON GRENNAN

These are big, ambitious, sometimes sprawling poems, rich in narrative and in detail, an autobiography of sorts, where the voyaging soul is concerned to find home and meaning in a dialogue between self and other. Like Saint Brendan, the author seems to understand that if home is where you set out from, home is also where you hope to find journey's end. Yet, if the title poem draws on the mythological, these poems are surely rooted in our century of migration and displacement, where identities are negotiated as much as given. It is the candid engagement with the difficult choices and trade-offs made in a search for some omphalos, some centre, in an ever more shifting world, which energises this collection.

—MOYA CANNON AND THEO DORGAN
Judges' citation, The Patrick Kavanagh Awards, 2008

"*As an avid reader of Irish literature, I found David McLoghlin's work to be fresh and unexpected, yet still worthy of inclusion in the great canon of poetry that is produced by his nation*"

—Mark Shaw
Natural Bridge journal

Crash Centre
David McLoghlin

salmonpoetry

Published in 2024 by
Salmon Poetry
Cliffs of Moher, County Clare, Ireland
Website: www.salmonpoetry.com
Email: info@salmonpoetry.com

Copyright © David McLoghlin, 2024

ISBN 978-1-915022-64-6

All rights reserved. No part of this publication may be reproduced or transmitted in any form or by any means, electronic or mechanical, including photography, recording, or any information storage or retrieval system, without permission in writing from the publisher. The book is sold subject to the condition that it shall not, by way of trade or otherwise, be lent, resold or otherwise circulated without the publisher's prior consent in any form of binding or cover other than that in which it is published and without a similar condition, including this condition, being imposed on the subsequent purchaser.

Cover & Title Page Photograph: JPR Williams, British Lions tour to South Africa, Final Test, 1974.
Reproduced courtesy of Colorsport / Colin Elsey
Cover Design & Typesetting: Siobhán Hutson

Printed in Ireland by Sprint Print

Salmon Poetry gratefully acknowledges the support of
The Arts Council / An Chomhairle Ealaíon

He who is silent is taken to agree;
he ought to have spoken when he was able to.
—Latin Proverb

In the middle of the road I had a stone
I had a stone in the middle of the road.
—Carlos Drummond de Andrade

For My Daughter
Íte Susan Ann McLoghlin

Contents

Dissociation	11
Talking About it	12
Blocking	14
The Drying Room	15
David Kieran	18
Hostage Walk	19
Pilot Fish	21
Mixed Media	23
Central Park Nocturne	24
The Room	25
A Time of Gifts	27
Three Person Sword	28
The Room (1998)	30
The Well	31
Stockholm Syndrome	32
Mosca	35
Private Rescue	36
Taking Everything	37
Nipples	39
Brucellosis	40
Dendrochronology	41
Clerical History	42
The Annals	43
Crone Mountain	44
Contact	45
Wolfsbane	46
Dear Reader	47

Black Holes	48
Orbital Resonance	49
The Senior Film	50
After the Room	51
Postern	53
Bones' Evidence	54
Trapped by Trees (2000)	56
Easter Vigil (2012)	58
Helpers	59
1 Corinthians 13	60
Porn King	61
Tom Crean Sings Sean-Nós At the Tiller in the Southern Ocean	64
Kamchatka	66
Crash Centre	67
Telling my Parents (2005)	70
Henry Street Garda Station: Reporting (2016)	71
Inter-Nuptials (2021)	72
Independent Commission for the Location of Victims' Silence	73
Blessing the Blind Man	75
Sandymount Strand, Nocturne	77
Notes	78
Acknowledgements	80
About the Author	82

Dissociation

During sex the mind drifts free
a gull—a gulf—
off the body's edge
back to the realm
of hurt, where the self
is an intense buzzing of bees
—insects, pins and needles:
helpers—maybe mice
frantically trying
to wake the young hero
from the sleep he was in,
has been in all these years
where something is happening
where someone is doing something
to him.

Talking About It

There was a world
tangled in my throat,
a tight singularity
that exploded
when words cut the container.

I said to a therapist
I think I was (—
abused.)

Walking yawed,
jellied.

Before, I had been
snow inside glass.

Particle collision.

The pinpoint
of truth from the tunnel
under the mountain
growing.

A great space is needed
when one starts to speak—
almost a whole other planet
for the pine forests around the castle
in the country where everyone
is sleeping.

*

Grotesque teenagers
paralysed in a growth spurt
came via the sly
interlocking thorns,

on through the courtyard
up into the room,
and kissed me.

When I woke, they were leaning over me,
mouth breathing. They said

You're not dead.
Get up.

Blocking

Drive to Mariabronn. The unnamed village serves
as base camp. Go in the gate—clatter of cattle grid—past the lodge
where Davey the groundsman lives. Without gaydar or proof,
Padge laughs, "He's your boyfriend, Glock!"
Matron's gate lodge latches the Back Avenue.
Motor up the Front Avenue, past cows and bucolics.
At the rhododendrons comes the turn: big reveal
of Normanesque castle on the hill, a fat tower either side,
Pax above decorative portcullis. Go through
to a lawn roundabout, our parents' Jags and Beemers
parked among Ford Escorts of the lay staff.
On your left, the school; on your right the monastery.
A sign: *Reception*. Beyond the two rooms where monks meet
visitors, the concept of *claustrum*, enclosure, begins.
Boys slouching there, Here, monks all in black,
robes sleek or shabby according to extent of eccentricity,
and crossing the semi-permeable membrane:
the teaching monks. Go up the hill to the church, past a fleet
of monastery cars. Near a fender, the monastery cat taking the sun.
Somewhere on the school side, the castle degenerates
into outbuildings: wooden kicking gym, boot room
—Victorian concept, a really good way to lose your shoes—
bike sheds, tunnel to the labs (Biology, Chemistry)
past them and past the cemetery, gravel declivity
to Chapel Lake, all lily pads. Beyond that
and the walled Biblical Garden, is an iron gate in a stone wall,
to uplands where I imagine myself Wordsworth striding the moors.
The way to the 99 steps to the Glen, and the Mass Rock
in a dripping forest, I forget it now.
                              Cut back through woods, and peer in
the window of a working artist, Henry Morgan, or stand below
the green corrugated gym beside the New Building,
where the cooler Sixth Years lean on the railing, roof smoking.
Showers are in the basement, near the Drying Room.
Most important to know, the time it takes
from *here* to *there*, New Building to *Reception*, at night,
with wet hair, to the door Fr. Narziss has just unlocked. Less
than five minutes. Here are the props, the troupe,
the blocking, the play.

The Drying Room

It was five minutes to the monastery
from the Senior showers—where I went
after supper, the day Fr. Narziss said:
"See you over in Reception at eight,
then. Have a shower, and make sure
that you're very clean." I was warm wax
for his seal, his signet, his appraising
smile during our first kiss. During
and after. Less than three months later,
I gave up rugby.

After training on the pitches in rain or sleet,
grit glittered in mud, and your own blood was in it.
Shorts forgotten a day or two
on the changing room floor were lost
in a ferment, like a slurry pit.

Gear got crunchy, coiling the wall pipes.
Like shoppers thinking aloud, Seniors said: "I need...
socks." And took a younger boy's. I almost liked it:
the natural filth of getting into dry, utterly dirty gear.
As if your jersey had shingles, its mud plaques
nervous-brittle, toasty against your back
standing in the Tenebrae of humming pipes.

On match day, the air stung with Deep Heat;
We faced each other—thoughtful, sitting,
vaselining then taping down our ears;
we taped our fingers, black tape among the white,
hands gritted for purchase, our wrists cooled
to the hilt in powdered bone. Our gum shields were in,
and we ourselves were weaponised,
had put on bronze greaves. Our gear was laundered,
our faces pale with adrenaline.

Sean Donovan genuflected for a private *Our Father*
then stood, slapping backs. Shouting started,
like an orchestra tuning towards a note.
Then we circled. Clasp. Touch.
—And go. The run down from the castle
was a flying column. I could hear the crowd,
metal studs on loose tar macadam,
the coaches saying, winded, around us

—"like a pack of wolves, Glen!"—
and the subs were running with us,
loyalty sparking up from the ground.
Young boys shouted our names, mothers stood
as we went by, their Hoplites.

I have at times wanted to go back, in order to remain
standing in my stained uniform among the mayhem
of school colours, the way I stood alone before a match
as if my own battle waited, and I was being cinched
into a breastplate by my grave squire, my kinsman,
a quarter inch of petrified mud-flakes under our boots
in the far corner of the Drying Room, where I have wanted
to stay in the radius of Sean's prayer.
On earth as it is in Heaven.

Narziss was saying, "Among the Athenians, inspiration
was an older man with a younger man: inspiring him—literally
inspiring. So, make sure that you're very clean." He kept
repeating "clean"—but jocular, and lulling. Only
now I can hear the italics. I was by myself
under the showerheads. I washed my hair,
and lathered my privates twice.
I didn't understand
he meant my anus.
I had oiled my ponytail, and over that unction
was wearing my favourite skull cap;
my Doc Marten eight-holes were on
and my Crombie swung open

like a First World War greatcoat. I went down
the flagstone passage, past Matron's circular room
at the tower's base, where our teachers took port
by the fire, nightly, I went down
the steep wooden stair to exit
under the arch that read *Pax*.

No one told me to go the lesser-used way, but I did.
I felt something—but so far off, it was years away
in the mind's snowfields, down in the core samples.
As my hand felt along the moss on the monastery wall,
the jerseys wrapping the pipes
ghosted for arms, holding on.

David Kieran

I remember David Kieran, who in boarding school
walked the unintentional chicken—head down,
elbows winging furiously against the sides
of his lungs. We laughed, doing the chicken-walk
behind him, not knowing it kept him from drowning.
He had to lie down twice a day on Nurse's table
for her to pummel loose the thick, grey sputum.
I wonder maybe he died of Cystic Fibrosis
before he could know romantic love.
I thought of him one night four thousand miles,
and years from there. Two years without touch,
as I again touched someone
—someone beautiful—I remembered David.

Hostage Walk

Before Lights Out, we'd be horsing around
when Fr. Narziss would come in,
"Hey!—Hey George! Stop that there now!"
There was no one by that name. Some scowled,
off to the side, at the antic ringmaster, or hurried
to finish pulling on their pajamas. But no one ever asked:
"What's a monk doing on the Fifth Year Floor
among half-naked 17-year-old boys at nine o'clock at night?"
He always left 10 minutes before our House Master
Fr. Andrew came to say, "What are you doing still up,
Mr. Beatty? To bed with you, sir. To bed."

Narziss drifted in several nights a week,
and in the gaggle that surrounded him
established enough credentials—"I was at Joan Baez...
Boston Common in '68. Oh, of *course*..."
—to draw us across to the monastery in a smaller group
to talk in the large Reception Room with the picture window
one day in autumn when crows were aloft.

We was my friend Tim, and me. Tim's hair
was almost white blond. Narziss loosened the collar,
boasting about opium and hashish, and perhaps
Herri Batasuna, or ETA, in Nationalist West Belfast.
"Oh, they were so handsome—long black hair—and so Basque."
Then he slipped in: "Did I tell you I'm gay?"
No teacher had been this honest.
I'd been reading *No One Here Gets Out Alive*, *Howl*
from City Lights, Baudelaire.
Someone said to Dad, "you let him read *Ginsberg*?"
and Dad was almost proud.
Narziss recommended so much.

We went back to the school side around four in the afternoon,
silent, clambering the blast crater.
We hadn't been in there that long. It's long.
First Years dispersed ahead of us like minnows,
hugging the reef; Robo moping artfully.
Tim never went back, and would never say: "You're excited
by Narziss, but—don't go back, Glock."

We know the hostage walk: monochrome streetscape,
some snow. Two figures walk towards opposing sides,
meet in the middle, and pass. On my way
to see Narziss three days later
I don't notice: he's booked the smaller room
this time, the one with no large window, only slit embrasures
in white walls. I see the enclosure, where monks
are passing—so contemplative, they are almost actors.

The day we walked back together, Tim made it
a normal day. People saw Tim, every day:
in the dorm, in the classroom.
No one asked: "where has David gone?"

Pilot Fish

The other priests
were pilot fish
though some didn't know
they were.
Did others know
through a feeling
through seaweed
and sea wrack
I see through the ruin
they didn't really see
the shark among them
ignored how often
I met you. One was
the receptionist
almost every time
the conduit
put the call through
Fr. ■
small simperer,
very discreet indeed:
"yes, Father Narziss?
...em, David McLoghlin
here to see you? Very good."
Then your feet, unerring,
coming down
the stairs
aspect of the boot boy
never quite masked
by lightness of tread
of the fat, and the campy.
Each time I met you,
went into the Reception Room
with the slit windows
three times a week to meet you;
when I came out

he would still
be there behind the desk
noting to himself how long
I had been in there
but still
saying nothing.

Mixed Media

It was in the Reception Room, on the left as you came into the white room—the painting with spikes, by Brother Benedict Tutty. There was a wood whorl, it seemed an eye, near the spikes, so that they could have been a beak. The spikes were blunt, but pressing hard enough could draw blood. I often ran my hand along them and said I wanted that. He said, "Yes! Oh, now, I love the wildness of it."

After walking across the reception area with me behind him, intoning things like, "yes. Thank you, Father," once he had closed the door behind us his face changed, his robe making a sweeping sound as he gathered speed, rushing me against the wall between the slit windows, where monks were passing. I stood as he knelt. I looked at the painting, disappearing into its eye.

Central Park, Nocturne

The living iguanas will come to bite the men who do not dream.

Federico García Lorca

Black trees—a little snow. People pause, deferring
to expensive dogs, maybe find a moment, like prayer,
breviary. From the reservoir, the buildings park-side seem
Angkor-Wat accretion, mud cities in Mali.
Gateway of oasis. *City of the wolf and the iguana.*
My childhood and future seem to have departed
to go jaunting, along empty pathways
under lamplight—electricity mimicking gas light—
in a park from home: the Retiro, maybe Phoenix Park.
Leaf preserved in grey ice. White ambergris.
Yellow hexagonals corona, come on high up,
hive-like, extending, silent. Night's calm black,
under surfacing.

The Room

It has taken years
to describe it: the room
at the end of thought's
corridor.

He used books like *Narziss and Goldmund*,
Giovanni's Room,
to get me to his
—barefoot, both of us carrying our shoes
past nameplates

Fr. Simon, Fr. Bonaventure,
Br. Michael, Fr. Kevin, Fr. Peter.

Ecclesiastical 8 o'clock
hush and lull in the enclosure, along the corridor
the rough hemp carpet
under our bare feet,
passing the red, unmoved Sacred Heart lights.
When we arrived
he opened the door
and I went inside. He said
*explore the dark
as if it was the interior of your self.*
I searched the walls,
his voice in the dark.

Then he turned on the light
and it was too bright.
Things since have been too bright.
(Drinking dims it.)

Then he said *take off your clothes
and lie down.*

I must have lain like a *toilette*.
Suddenly he was there in the doorway
in a kimono,
his skin so white
the belly straining past the profile
of the kimono

the way sausage strains
against the skin;
the flesh discoloured on his legs
male, but hairless;
purplish, mottled on the shins.

He wiped me
with a damp, lukewarm face cloth
face the sheet, as if
before a procedure.

There is a second
of snow and static

then it stitches
into us lying on the bed
talking like lovers,
as if—*after*.

A Time of Gifts

It was the beautiful John Murray edition,
cover in colour pencil, sun on snow,
illuminated mountains of *Mittel Europa*,
Patrick L. Fermor as a teenager, setting out
to walk from Holland to Istanbul in 1933.
In our bedroom, a port city
that had turned away from the fecund sea,
I shouted at my Spanish girlfriend,
"He *had* his time of gifts—mine was stolen!"
She winced and was confused.
When I was alone, I tore the book in two.

Three Person Sword

Books on China
and "The Japans"
lined his room, including
the erotics of the Samurai.
"I love the loincloth. The way it *bisects*
the ass," he said.

The Samurai
could cut you
clean in half, from right
carotid to left
hip

        if you were a peasant,
perceived to not have bowed
low enough to the *daimyō*
then one of them would step forward.

The poise, stillness lake-mind
necessary to make that cut
—like the flow of a brush
once put to paper,
a decision that must be lived with
from beginning to end—
nodded at by those watching:
the beauty of terror

then they would have left
to feast on roe and sea urchins,
clean in their robes
after floating in the steam
with the lotus,
leaving your family to collect
your trunk:
still kneeling.

A sword hummed in him
like rimmed glasses
rubbed to a screeching.

Those old swords still hang
dappled by canted sunlight
in museums in Dublin.

When I was seventeen, I said to my teacher,
"I'm curious about what it's like
to kiss a man." He said,
"you can kiss me
—if you like."

The Room (1998)

When you laid your hands
on my nipples as you went down
on me, your palms
had eyes
           something was beginning
to crowd my breathing, rationing
it into smaller
parcels. I opened my eyes.
Dark coming
through the ceiling. I couldn't see,
something too present, pore
memory, and I started to scream
turn on the light!

You stumbled up, naked,
knocking over a lamp. You didn't know
the room yet. We were still learning
each other. *Where is it?* you pleaded
into the screaming,
a desperate outline against the wall.
Then we were kneeling,
deliver us from evil
over and over, as you held me
in the weird light.

      *

Switch to bulb takes years
to arrive in context. But it isn't sight
that activates it. It's the sound
of blind-scrabbling, chipboard
splintering under your nails.
The sound is me: flailing
the wall in the dark
as he waits beside the light switch.

The Well

The heart's gone to seed: crusty and aqueous, like algae
you could walk on—scabs of bad bloom. I need to clear
the surface, to the way a fisherman watches weeds fly
in the sluices of the mill race. I find it off the main flow, half a mile
into the woods from the footbridge. It has been unattended.
I take branches out, then leaves—sometimes veined sunlight,
thin branching flame. Waiting for water to rise, I polish the edge
of a thought, like clearing away sleep. I don't think
of what Finn did. There's no guarantee a salmon will rise.
In clearings there's sky in earth. On the surface it's patient
—like a heron's eye, and gives back watery trees,
registers the whooping of the swans—here again from Iceland
nervous on the river. Any step closer, and they clear
to wingbeats.

Stolkholm Syndrome

Niall Noígíallach: Old Irish, "having nine hostages,"
pronounced *noí*, nine; *gíall*, a human pledge or hostage;
the possessive suffix *-ach*.

A man on the subway in shorts
and white ankle socks
brings you back,
brings back visiting you in Belfast.
A nick in the shower
and your little toe had gone black.

Diabetic, you were strangely careless
though you were careful
in every other way.
You wrote Thank You cards
the morning after the party. Your hand
never left the line.
Reeling in, you were never careless with me
—a gel Novocained the hook.
No one could smell your sweat on me.

With others you wore manners
like a translucent membrane.
You stole food as I prepared it
once, visiting me a day
when I was wrapped
in a long thesis without headway
—Barry Wasserman's rental,
The Old School House
two miles from the Cliffs of Moher.

You gobbled half the chorizo
meant for the meal.
When I told you *stop it*, you danced
the magpie, mocking
stop it, stop! and would not stop
it, the beak tip starting to poke.

After lunch, you napped, regal.
I sat on the front step, fuzzy,
an unhoused nervous system
looking down on Lahinch,
Liscannor Bay, the mapping
of early summer.

After an hour, your apology:
a touch on my shoulder
(—inserted a line, whisper
of a pump,
parasite proboscis
piping away blood).

Post-op in Belfast, you lay fatly on the couch
in your tracksuit bottoms
and baby-white ankle socks.

I said, "I'd like to see it."
Thrilled, you said, "I *love*
how you're fascinated by wounds."

You peeled back the dressing.
I remember nothing
about the stump.
Poor Tom Thumb
—not there at all.

> I do remember.
> —Like meat, a marbling:
> a congealed gel-surfacing.

None of it visible once you put on
the sock. We stayed in
the whole weekend. Your sister
waiting on us hand and foot.

I didn't go out to see Belfast.
I was safe in your house. It was
pleasant, your suburbs ringing
around me.

*

I am thinking of West Clare,
quick cloud shadows on pasture
May sun on clean hay-gold,
and me, separate from sunlight,
from Ireland
from history.

You are
—*say him*—
▪▪ ▪▪
defrocked from the Order
of ▪▪ ▪▪

You controlled the postern gate.
How many of us there were
is a stair into darkness.

Niall of the Nine Hostages
was from Ulster. People
boast they are of his lineage.

Only the raptor is recorded.
We don't know their names.

I see them in the shadows
under my eyes.
I see my school friends.
Some of them were hostaged too.
I don't know who.

Mosca

The name on a donor's cheque,
Antoinette Elizabeth Volpe, brings back
The Globe, the bear pit, *Volpone*.
In student days at Queens, you played
Mosca, the parasite servant.
They gave you a hood and greasepainted
your face: one side white, the other black.
You loved how no one saw 'til it was too late.
"In rehearsal I'd change my blocking,
stand in the shadows with my hood up.
When they saw me, the actors would jump."

Private Rescue

There is a box room rescuers have identified
and are working towards, the crews chipping
industrial diamond blades on the copper layer
of years—to meet it, and sledge it through.
The boy inside notices the wallpaper starting
to ripple, and fracture.

There were headlines under the bowl
on the trays he slotted through:
Agreement Scuppered, or *Terror Continues
Unabated*. We had an economy of touch.
He was my country. My body was starlings
still coming home to roost.

No silver-foil blanket after the marathon,
or way stations of water. No flag of nation
raised in the rubble.

Taking Everything

The writing teacher says:
"we believe it. But
what's an image for
taking everything?"

                It would be his eyes
glazed, up close, a quarter
of a second before he kissed
me, lips shucking over oyster shell
—though my shell was soft—slurping me
down and in—it would be his eyes
almost crazed for an intelligent man
who had studied theology and come up
in the world from the Falls Road
during Internment
to be among the Brothers

where he pulled the hairs
around my nipples
—no hair on my *chinny-chin-chin*—
an eager tugging
almost a ripping, his lips billowing—
not a sigh, but an impulse out,
an imposition. If you did this, you would ask
hesitant permission. "Baby, will we act a—
rape fantasy"? You wouldn't do this
to your pupil

they were so dilated, not seeing me. I contracted,
and froze: ice to be shaved

absorbed, then disappear. He was always sober,
though his face and eyes were glazed with a layer
like lamb fat, his lips chewing as if eating
—but not seeing me—like someone at a feast
who isn't hungry, an addict

bingeing the table.
Plunder and ravish
the swan, and quail,
and their quail eggs, the whole Tudor
beauty of it—does not know
it is beautiful.

Nipples

As if excited by what he was getting
away with, he leered—and, what was I
going to do, anyway? Go outside
into the corridor, where other priests were passing,
tell someone about it?—
he tugged the hairs around my nipples
as if playing an instrument
through systolic gesture:
curly piano wire
pulled straight.
One bunching set of fingers
would tug, leer; then
slacken
as the other hand tugged. Leer
of lips and eyes
—simian, intelligent.
When I said *that hurts* (through gesture,
turning away) the face
came closer, close spittle,
imitation child-voice:
"it—*hu-rts*."
My teacher
seemed transformed.
I didn't understand
—he had unveiled himself.

Brucellosis

"Oh, Ann, would you *look*. Milk from our own cows,"
Nurse Supple said to Mum in a back corridor one afternoon
near the kitchens where *wenches* were: local women
we said stank. Nurse scooped frothy cream, a whole inch.
The churns were beaded metal, and had travelled
less than a mile. The herd had only eaten monastery grass:
no need to be pasteurised. An aborted calf was the first sign.
Then the first boy fell ill, then another, and it was
a scandal. Parents railed, threatening action. The local farmers
were angry—the carelessness, the entitlement of it—fearful
it would spread. Someone said one boy had it, but hadn't developed
symptoms. Someone said, "those boys might have it for life."
We didn't know who had it. After their parents stopped speaking
out, there were murmurs about compensation. *Milk Sickness,
Chumble Fever, Contagious Abortion, Satan's Fever, Fist of Mercy*
—parallel to the named world, I was travelling to a place
where images keep coming back. Churn, milk, froth:
tiny bubbles were contained inside Fr. Nariziss's foreskin,
like a culinary foam: jellied caviar, spume of translucent cells.
I saw it as I went down, thinking, *we've only just got here*.
But he is benignly uninterested, flaccid, smiling to himself.
It is the night I lose the time between him wiping me—the warm
facecloth impregnated with essential oils—and *later*: us lying together
with lassitude. I am spacey, and calm. What I thought was a second's
splicing might be thousands of missing frames.
My questions come to term. That clear foreskin roe:
pre- or post-cum? Are haemorrhoids
memory? My mind keeps glitching along the crack.

Dendrochronology

I live underneath the scriptorium.
I perceive sunlight   hear birdsong
through him   in him.

He is the only aperture.
I, an epoch in microfiche
hair on a fiddlehead

its genital stem—*f* uncoiling
in time lapse in the margin
of his lectern. I can't be touched

by sun dials   or the shadows
from the markers of history.
I am unleavened

dissolving in his mouth.
I live under a fern curlicue.
In the word forest   I am less

than the faintest tree ring.
From the room under the room
walled-in inside him I hear

the First Years the new boys
and him   like a prophet
going out to walk among them

Clerical History

During the Penal Laws, when Catholics were outlawed in their own country, the Mass moved—and with it "the masses"—to glens and wild places: outcroppings known later as Mass Rocks, where they knelt for communion on drenched grass and brambles. There was one on the school grounds: at the bottom of the Glen, via the 99 steps. Priests were our people: from us, returning to us—their ground and receivers: every mother proud to have "*a son, a priest.*" Even in the late '80s, it held. He had made his mother proud. The collar dealt with traffic cops—"*Christ!* would you look at the ass on that one?"—and got best flirting waiter service, the old women giving way as he swept past, back from the toilet. During dessert we said, without fail, grave, "would you have another *Benedictine*, Father?" then tittered at the in-joke. Pricking into choler, he said: "I'm sure we haven't heard that one before."

The Annals

It is recorded that the Northmen
first raided Lindisfarne and Iona
then from fen and estuary followed
the soft inland waterways into Ireland
where they sacked monasteries
for their fine worked things, plucking
jewels like eyes from the covers of books.
The Annals of Innisfallen records
their taking Etgal the abbot of Skellig
Michael for ransom in 823, who died
of hunger at their hands.   At the Abbey
you kept the annals, penmanship
better suited to the old vellum. I doubt you
mention me, even in marginalia.
A skin of bad touch. A gouge pen.

Crone Mountain

—After Lorca

Moon—chrome tear on the cheekbone
of Cruach Mhárthain—seeping through
skylight, roof tiles and concrete,
swimming the room: like a tide pouring out
in spate, the stranger I hold back
from watching daily, new planets—Titan,
Europa, travelling at speed over water. Moon.
Madness of spring tides. Stillness in the head
like a hurricane. The bed is a white space
that is travelling, travelling. My body's a cut-out
on the Sea of Tranquility—mercury dappling
—making it beautiful to the one who isn't here:
tall, dangerous white lady—outside the door now,
turning the key. Eyes: crescents of glacier,
breasts of polished tin.

Contact

—for Adrienne

On the bus to the writing conference
she touches the smashed glass
with her forefinger—the fifty-year-old
housewife ex-lawyer: writing for herself,
now, she says.

Sunlight runs inside the fracturing
as she explores what's been ruined,
as if, touching a Man o' War,
expecting to be cut
by sharp water,
she withdraws her hand
shocked at how soft it is.

Read me *Rapunzel*,
the wife coveting rampion
from the witch's garden; read me
Beauty and the Beast again—
it takes 100 days
to trust her with the ugliness.

I want you to touch me. I'm so tired
and have laid myself down on the ground for you.

Wolfsbane

—The year of *touching the teenager* over,
the mind fuck only beginning. College weekends
visiting my parents, you came over for dinner
most often when Dad was away on business. A thread
of cream still swirling after you took out the spoon
you gestured—phrasing air—"your father. Mmm... Oh,
don't get me wrong. He's so sensitive. But, he travels a lot—
doesn't he?" Mum served us dessert by the open fire,
her best Waterford crystal. I was fume of juniper
in your gin, paperweight in your palm. Hyena, wolf—
whatever metaphor I give you, I had to eat my way out
of you: Goliard, Billy Bunter disporting in Tuck Shop;
three spoonfuls of Type 2 in every cup, bellyful of stone.
Everything went in: cucumber sandwich, the crusts cut,
jelly babies, adolescent penis, digestive biscuits,
the aged prime fillet Mum ordered for *the priest's visit*,
a child's limbs. Finally, I had to stop living inside you,
seeing through your eyes.

Dear Reader

I was liquid,
to be added to his.
That was what I was for.
Not even metaphor.

This is the birth of the static
in me now.

I leap between channels.
When you finish reading
you change the transmission.
But he stays broadcasting
at least a day
until the receptor goes silent.
He's still active, somewhere.

Black Holes

Time bends me back—in there—again.
I remember you reminiscing: "I called the roll.
'*David McLoghlin?*' And a boy in the back row
blushed. I said to myself, '*Ah*. What is it
that makes him embarrassed when someone
says his name?'"

When you said, "you can kiss *me*—if you like,"
your lips had a plushness, your eyes bright
with something you were telling only yourself,
almost as if you were humming.

Orbital Resonance

In fifth and sixth year, and for 14 years after, we were binary stars. "Just like *Harold and Maude*! Or Narziss and Goldmund," you loved to say. The truth was, you were primary, my side of our figure 8—me—the planetoid—shrinking almost to nothing. At the end, when I released from the mass of your folding, then I knew the shearing: eddies of awesome gravitation. Once I "cleared your neighbourhood", astronomically speaking, after years I could move from being a dwarf planet, and see you clear: so much insubstantial, roiling around a pin prick. I sense you still. And know: if I hadn't told the school, you'd still be strutting, positioning yourself for the orbit of young stars: the mysterious beginning, being *seen* by a mentor, the twining. Then the pinion, and the seizing.

The Senior Film

"As newborn babes, desire the rational milk without guile..."
                                                          1 Peter, 2:2

After *The Name of the Rose*, we were on a quest to doppelgäng
our teachers. In the dorm—glimmer of moon on tuck
of 20 cocoons—the crosstalk was an excited quadrangle:
"who's *that* monk like?" "Shag?" "The Fod?" "No. It's Con-Dom! And
that one's Double-0-Kev!" We were thrilled by the Quasimodo one;
the one with lids of glaucoma; the ones with forehead warts
and warted forefingers. But we needed a *doppel* for Father B.,
who during Sunday Mass pushed his white mane back
along a streak of nicotine, a frog in his throat,
like Seán MacBride, a bog man who'd grown up in France.
We even found a double for a monk whose wattle quavered—we said—
because he'd been stretched on the rack like taffy.
But no one mentioned the one who was *contra naturam*,
or compared him to any of our own.
He was quiet and obese,
shrieked at mice in the scriptorium—
white as beluga, or narwhal, he died
from licking poison: a page turner.
Many of us flocked to you when you danced by, Pied-Piping;
others—like Nick and Robo—watched
with a look of sour milk, without saying the source
of the spoilage.
You said to me: "Davy, the most erotic moment *isn't*
when Adso the novice and the village woman
make love in front of the stove"—the fire's core
almost liquid—"it's when the abbot kisses Br. William,
the Sean Connery character, welcome
full on the lips. Notice how his eyes are open. Now *that's*
erotic." Your eyes open
during the kiss.

After the Room

After creeping along
the red corridor that was like
being inside a blood vessel
in a Sacred Heart
the stockinged, steady swish
of your surplice rushing behind me,
we stood in the Reception area—
you directly beneath the arch
that marked the *enclosure*
your feet just behind the line.
I stood in profane space, coy,
thinking myself Rimbaud.
In the dark, your hood up,
you smiled—

Then Father Mark came in
a side door.
We didn't move, stayed
facing each other.
He wrote the textbook
for Leaving Cert History
—*Modern Ireland: 1850-1950*—
but can't corroborate
because he's dead now.
As if scripted, we said
Hello, Father,
you, particularly mocking,
then he was gone.

I am gone—
out the side door
I called *the postern gate*.

Crossing to the school
for the last 10 minutes

of the Senior Film
I stood beside Father Andrew
who glanced at me.
I savoured the taste,
sticky—
children's glue
bonding my lips.

Postern

On my way back
to the school, I turned—
there in the door
before you closed it
was your face.

Bones' Evidence

In the new monastery library
passing the annals
—you were *keeper of what happened*—
you gestured at that Japanese-Swedish sense
of balance: house integrated
into forest. Looking out the long windows
it was strange at 33 to see myself—repositioned

closer to the teenager
who disobeyed the forestry *No Entry* sign
to find silence on the bench in the clearing:
sunlight through walls of Cedars of Lebanon.
I came back carrying a mug
of cold water from the aquifer.
You drained it each day.

As we sat now in the new
guesthouse—earnest young people
in Birkenstocks and wool socks
deferring to your black robes and hood
I noticed through half a conversation
you had been praising me.
Then I noticed I'd been drinking it in.

The bag above my arm stopped
and in the pause—like a patient
reaching up and around—
out of my mouth, I started to remove
wadding.
               The drip would not
go back in. In the arm's instep
the lips of the slit mouth
started to mumble.

White to off-porcelain
to old ivory
under the creosote
like teeth after a taking,
chattering.

Palimpsest scratcher, you hid
in my body.

Trapped by Trees (2000)

Cosy in the same parlour as before, my mind snips
the tubes between sensation and memory
—his face avid, almost billowing—
this time I'm an "Old Boy" in my late 20s—Goldmund,
or returned *Glenstallion*—driving my mother's car
on a Learner permit. Receptionist's nod, grave,
half-comic inclination of old teachers stopping to chat:
Narziss a pace back, witnessing, half-smiling
as Fr. Simon mocks: "What are *you* doing
back here, again, *McLoghlin*?"
The affection acknowledges: I've passed
beyond their remit, though am still tied.
        Wild rain, monks in the rear-view gather
skirts and run for the castle. Halfway along
the Front Avenue: a big oak's down, circumference
to my windscreen top. A screeching
five-pointer in second, branches bristling
blood trees in the optic nerve: *No worries,
route home via the Back Avenue*, but another big one's
fallen in the space of stopping. Fairytales
would connote a mysterious *funnelling*
towards some end manipulated by castle
     or Manor House. I walk back up towards
twinkling medieval lights. Monks gather matronly,
concerned but ambivalent about external disturbance
so close to Compline. Narziss gestures all that bullshit away
with a hand chop. "Give him the phone." Pursed lips hand
over the Bakelite I used to dial him—185—100 times.
I ring my parents. "You'll stay for dinner,"
Narziss says, "then we'll get you on your way."
     I process in with the monks and some guests
—pre-novice try-outs conservative in civvies—
listen to a reading from the podium
—some Desert Father, or obscure Apostle—
everyone fast-spooning soup in silence.

We stand for prayer, process out. Buoyed,
I walk down. Someone's freed me
with chainsaws. I drive through the trees,
the road home routes me round the avenues:
my Möbius for the foreseeable years ahead.

Easter Vigil (2012)

—for Adrienne

First the church went absolutely black, then
the fire vault was lit—baptismal font, fontanelle—
shadows licking the faces of the good priests, parents,
trim, male New York couples, baby in a stroller
—corpulent man with cropped hair, hawk eyes,
two rows across, *near children*—a sick flash
it's him. I am a faulty, damaged prism. No.
I shake him from my eyes.
Love, it's been a hard belay, to come here again—
climbers tracking across a face,
searching for hand holds, a path up.

Helpers

You promised me, and you said a lie to me,
...You promised me a thing that is not possible

("Donal Óg", translated by Lady Gregory)

There are things you've never worn: the suit
that stitches rows of dragon's teeth—seedlings—
the gloves made of the skin of a fish
that walked from Lough Corrib, only apparent
in western isle moonlight, the shoes made
from the skin of a child's favourite piglet
that gave itself freely. That must be the meaning
of submission. A pocket square
of crocodile tears betrayed them. The suit,
the gloves, the shoes, confer at night—Bremen voices
in the cupboard out in the hall that has no visible
door. *When will we be worn for the good fight?*
The battle's already here. We are a good armoury.
An army of little men will spring out of the ground.

1 Corinthians 13

You shook your head and said: "Marriage? You'll never
marry. Oh, you'll have girlfriends, certainly, but—marriage?
No." I never questioned you, but in the days before, I saw
what you had said was straw-filled. Oil coating brass.
A dirty chrism. At your core, you were a clanging bell.
We chose Corinthians. My cousin Richard, our priest, said
—"this is the only one of the seven where you administer
the sacrament yourselves." And when he read *the greatest
of these is love,* I knew it was the truth.
I didn't think of you on my wedding day.

Porn King

Procrastinating, afternoon to evening behind a daytime curtain
goes fuzzy and white, hopscotching inside the honeycomb:
TV with spag bol (two-and-a-half portions), Kenco instant;
two beers, three; then carpet-burn: the mood bath so warm
and soft it verges on fibreglass, like being wrapped in cotton wool.
A finger from a saint's hand—or some other wanker—
a relic from the days of dial-up. 1995 and 1996,
spent disassociating.

*

It takes so long to load I mutter "bollox", and go to make tea
instead. In my absence, a woman's head smiles
waiting for her body to arrive. The modem hisses, *Krrs. Krrsss*:
the sound of something coming down the line. It recalls
a documentary's solemn imagined "end via black hole"
where I elongate like taffy in the event horizon,
and then am obliterated, pixel by pixel.

*

Before we knew about webmail, and put our trust
in hosts out on the ether, my parents paid for ann-, brian-,
ruth-, david-, rebecca- and marc-: all snug @islandhouse.iol.ie.
When email was local, visiting my parents I got itchy
for something half-decent, and used Dad's computer to subscribe.
Back in Dublin I got the call: "David, I got this strange email from"
—here, he italicised—"XXX.com." Pause. "Your *mother* feels
pornography is degrading to women." My head bowed,
I nodded, a dripping tap. After that, for a while
my sister's boyfriend called me
The Porn King.

*

I was 15 when Ricki Roche liberated a mag, *Oui*,
out of his father's arsenal. Ten of us crowded round
the naked couple on the bonnet of a yellow Ferrari. She:
amazing, dyed blonde; he, only relevant in equipment terms
—incredible positioning, and nothing for the imagination.
Over the coming weeks, one by one we crept back to the dorm
to tear pieces for wank fodder, until there was nothing left
but bad prose and ads for vibrators.

*

A year later, me and Fr. Narziss are sitting in the monastery
guest kitchen, just beyond the lintel marking the enclosure.
The distance from sacred to secular is like Zeno of Elea
slicing space, like meat you can see through, or Occam's razor.
Narziss's legs are crossed under the belted black robe: Friar Tuck
in black polyester socks and Birkenstocks. He says, "I've something
here to show you, David." And from a manila folder, out of a sheaf
of papers that could have *Nihil Obstat* all over them,
he hands me a magazine with naked men
smiling on the cover.

"*Well*, we'd been discussing your sexuality, so I thought
this might help. What do you think? Do you like that?"
"I don't know," I say. I am with my best friend.
Why am I afraid? As the pages turn, bulbs explode,
paparazzi or pornographers crowding round,
jostling for a piece of me. I go into another room, multiverse
of cotton wool and string theory. There's an alarm ringing
somewhere, but the tongue's been taken from the bell.

*

At a party, years later—who is it that counts the gaps
among the years?—I gather some friends, go up the spiral stairs
to Dad's study, input a password on a site.
I don't even ask, *why am I doing this?*

Everyone acts naturally. Now I imagine the happy couples
asking each other later that night,
"why do you think he showed us pornography?"

    *

It has happened during pillow fuckery:
close to the laptop screen, optic nerve and eye
lie horizontal, outside my body
like Leaving Cert Biology diagrammes: something lopped
off but still connected.
Her face is close to the camera. Our eyes meet.
Help me.

Tom Crean Sings Sean-Nós at the Tiller in the Southern Ocean

And there were still 18 days until they would cross South Georgia
—something that was impossible: to cross crevasses
in perpetual snow with a biscuit each and ice for water
to make you thirst more, bare equipment, clothes
that were falling apart on the three of them—Worsley, Shackleton
and Crean—when increasingly they could have sworn
there was a fourth man with them in the dream stumble, days until
they walked into the whaling station at Stromness Bay, unrecognisable,
sooted from blubber smoke on Elephant Island, and five months
on the pack ice that travelled the Weddell Sea after *Endurance*
went down. Two boys ran from them in terror, shouting
"Strange men are coming!" because they were coming
from the interior, a direction from which no one comes.
But there were still 18 days in the ice flood—jerry-rigged, timbers
and nails salvaged out of the lifeboats, navigating 800 nautical miles
to reach the island by a sun sighting, on days when there was none,
waves coming at them uninterrupted from Cape Horn: sky blockers,
to come out of despair to save the men who were sheltering
under the boats on the ice shingle, snatching sleep in the rock ballast
that cut the ribs of dreams, days you had to chip your hand off
the tiller when your watch was over.
                            When Tom Crean took the tiller
he started to sing. They said later they thought he had invented
the song, that it was an invented language, or no language.
They didn't understand the words, did not know there were words
or that it was a source that means *old way*. But when waves froze
at the frothing point, they wanted the song to go on. It went on
into continuance, though no one knew where they were,
relying on Worsley to find a sliver of island
in the Southern Ocean sailors feared in boats bigger than theirs,
it went on, though there was no one to hold the singer's hand
and wind it slowly, as reminder that some bonds still hold
this side of the journey into the song, though

he was as far as you could get from Annascaul, he sang in the bilge
of a scuppering boat, sang—maybe—as he crawled forward
to scrape ice off the sails. He sang into the crone,
like the war pipes, or an orca fin breaking surface, dissonance
and harmonium, the way a piper will open the drone and keep playing
along the difficult angles—the chanter, the elbow a lung
of breath-steadiness, the side vents mouths for the voices
—like a tide breaking up through the blow holes, or an army
or home—not harmony, but ululation, singing through a wound,
singing through. Fantastic vowels, dreaming his people
lining up like waves behind him.

Kamchatka

In a film about Argentina in the time of the Disappeared,
a father says to his son: "Kamchatka is where you go: to resist."
When Justin, Niall and I played *Risk*
in Niallo's caravan in the dunes of Ventry Strand,
I used to try for Kamchatka: just so I could give that line.
I withdrew there, volcanic and isolate, when I lost
beyond the game. I had ceded almost an entire territory
to live in the last uncorrupted cell, which was still
connected, if I wanted, via a land bridge, a single
black line. I vacated Ireland when he touched me.

From the Skellig to the Causeway,
I want my country again.
I want the sentinel places to wake:
Mizen, Erris, Bloody Foreland, Carnsore.
Pass the Fastnet on your right, north-north east
on a 32-point windrose. Unjam the wind.
We'll sit in the Wishing Chair,
spines against basalt, and start to reimagine.

Crash Centre

He should run as straight as possible. Ideally a gap will appear in the defense, but even if caught he is likely to have broken the advantage line and will be able to create a situation for good second-phase possession.

—JPR Williams, *How the Lions Won*

A centre should master the simple arts of rugby and recognise his role as a supporter of movement. He should be willing, in other words, to do more running in support than in possession.

—Mike Gibson, *How the Lions Won*

I used to straighten the line the instant
I entered it: the spin pass from John Fitz
at Fly Half to Jan, the First, then me
at Second Centre—there was our tendency
to drift, but I took the ball head-on:
not counter angle or scissors move,
but because the others were imperceptibly
drifting towards touch with every pass,
when I took it straight it was a cleaving.

"You're what they call a *crash centre*,"
my father said. It was JPR Williams
counter attacking against the All Blacks
with no gum shield, bizarre Boer War
sideburns, his socks round his ankles,
unafraid as a holy fool, it was Trevor Ringland
pretty boy blond, cowled hair of a novice,
but taking the ball into contact, and through, it was
the one direct thing I knew to do.

Sometimes my opposite number would be
horizontal in air
trying to tackle me, his hands clattering
off my thighs as I went through was sound
barrier, triggering the g-force of *they will*

not stop me,
decisive as a hand-off to the face—
will not take me down.

Sometimes I made the line myself.
Once, after carving 40 yards from our own 22,
attacking out of defense—*made shit of them*—
the only man left ahead of me the Full Back
—a boy, in all that space—
the confidence to finish it deserted me,
and another ran in for the try.

———

Whenever Father Narziss appeared on the touch
line in his black robe, he attracted apostles.
All through 1990, he side stepped
and wove, wheedling: "but you're a *poet*!
Rugby's so boring. I don't understand team sports.
Wouldn't it be better if, when they caught someone,
like the Bacchante in Greek times, instead
of just tackling them, they tore him apart?"

I left the team in fifth year to go and talk
to him three times a week about Rilke.
Ravens wheeled from the battlements
as I walked across to the monastery.
Half past three until five in the afternoon
was the lull: dead time, touching time
in the Reception Room.

———

I had loved our wings, Dan or Andrew,
running in clean, untackled,
knowing: *I was the extra man.*
My shins grass-matted, a stud dent,
blood-trickle among the mud,
and he: completely clean.
I wanted to be that classy winger,
but I was proud to do the one thing I could do.

When I crashed the gap, when I took the tackle
—sustained by it, almost—slowing, but keeping
going, giving high knee-hits,
studs cutting the air, as more and more
of them dragged me down, I felt the wind
of support coming

our forwards: Egan the leggy Open Side
Flanker, who scythe-tackled at ankle level
and was always first to the breakdown
shouldering me, slotting in, driving the maul,
the bind of Fabo's stone hands
then Nuge the Number 8, the Locks,
and at last Henry, the Hooker

and the Props, Sean and Psycho,
out of the engine room core: first in and last out
of every scrum, picking themselves out of the mud
all day long to find you.
I found myself at the centre
of a human shield, what it might have been
in the war turtle of Leonidas—
in the steam and maelstrom
our heads close, touching, as if planning,
a hand binding you, a hand ripping back the hands
that reached for you in the dark, an urgent voice,
pass it back, or: *on your left, Glocky—Left side!*
We connected to our own kinesis,
harnessed it, and drove forward.

My job was: even if you are tackled, taken out—
if you can't break through, create space
for someone else, for the winger
or pass it back inside to Jan,
never give a hospital pass
but be the continuity, the place
where a negative inheritance
stops. That was what I had loved:
ceasing lateral drift. Straighten the line.

Telling My Parents (2005)

Hurried consultation in the hall, spleen
in the throat. "Well, we're going back
to Dublin, right?" "Shit. I've got to tell them now."
She nods, pale, hugs me quick, I go towards
my parents' room: tasteful pastels, the off-white
and yellow spectrum. "Hi there?" "In here, Dave,"
my mother's voice. One is in the bathroom, the other
in the dressing room: the walk-in floor-to-ceiling mirrors
with mahogany surrounds. Mum finishes up and comes out
as Dad turns to receive me: half smiles on their faces,
their son, down on a visit—to change the future past
with this. Just as I say, "I need to tell you something,"
Ella, my niece, a toddler, bursts in:
"I need you Gwanny!" just as I am saying,
"Narziss, he..."   The cinema pause is true
so stilted in script. Mum's face falling,
Ella saying again "Granny! I *need* you!"
"Sorry Dave, I have to," almost her relief to not hear it
first-hand. Dad: "What were you saying, Dave?"
"Narziss, he..." I can't
get to the verb. Dad's eyes focus.
Almost in lawyer mode, he slows, chooses each word:
"he *got* to you, didn't he?"
I nod, then step into his arms.

Henry Street Garda Station, Reporting (2016)

I shout at my mother. She flinches. And I see how she is 70.
She's mixed up copies and originals. Nothing naked, just photos
testifying to frequent proximity: him in his 40s, me at 17. "I asked you
to keep them separate—and you couldn't do it!" She stood
for me—I couldn't—light lasering iris, continuously facing
his satisfaction feeding onto the tray—bitter for her,
to digest the spoilt years of hospitality.
The eve of it, Mum and Dad chat over trussed
pork steak and roast potatoes, as if the transatlantic visit is normal.
The Spanish red textures my dissociation, and I see
them, tired, handing off the baton for the last time. As I sprint
for the line, they stand, heads bowed, hands on their knees.
The next morning she drops me at Henry Street. The redbrick bristles
with antennae: armed response and anti-gangland.
She speeds off. This isn't her Limerick, she isn't dropping
her son here. He's on his way to Nancy Blake's for pub grub
with Max, or to *Leonard's* for a jumper by Tricot Marine. She's on the way
to Brown Thomas for a blow dry. Walking up the steps, one step short
of the Four Courts, something arcs between the polarities of the body
entering the lobby, I am a singularity tainting the day
where an elderly cleaning lady, townie accent, is joshing
the Ban Garda on duty, and the couple in tracksuits
is getting their baby's first passport. "Ah, isn't she gorgeous?"
I'm ashamed of what I come carrying. I reach for friends.
Be with me now. 26 years. One exhale. My turn. I ask
for detectives by name. Two of them come, solicitous, serious: *David?*
Their accents are disparaged, and needed. I am asking the City, me
of elite, of Limerick County, am asking the City—
the boys we played against: Munchins, Ard Scoil, Clements, South Hill,
the girls of Laurel Hill, the boys and girls of Crescent
—to help me.

Inter-Nuptials (2021)

It's complicated clearing a mine field while negotiating
a living document, tracking change as we Venn Diagram, entwine
currencies, and everything else invested. Poor plaintiff,
I say: "I give so much time and space to others I've nothing left
for myself!" "That's not my fucking problem! Take care
of yourself! If not for your sake, then for mine, your daughter's."
You're right. I offer things you haven't asked for, pass
the unnecessary salt, then resent your *no*. You're the best
arguer I've ever met. I mean that in a good way. The source
of your cold "Business Mode" is your Dad waking you at 3 a.m.
to troubleshoot financial problems when you were five.
I make others responsible, problems I create, or inherited, give away
control to stay victim. I'm angry with you without knowing why.
I know why, don't want to know. Get out of my space get out of my—
you take too much room in the bed, your feet blocks from the icehouse
laid on my ankles, or love cats tunnelling for warmth. If I wasn't
so angry, it'd be cute. Instead: "You take three quarters
and keep extending," into Poland. "But, you keep retreating
to your side, so I follow." Then I realise. How stupid I am,
how like a porcupine going nuclear shooting quills of *noli tangere*—
you're my wife, not Narziss, who said it wouldn't happen.
Well, we happened. How often we reduce to talking shop,
kid logistics, but last night, our first date in how long—you scheduled it—
I rediscovered you, sitting across, Cork City below us, early January
of New Year lights. I wiped condensation from my face
like wiping mud layers, wrinkles. I know I've been hiding, cringed
that time you said, "the last time we—months ago..." and: "my best years are..."
I know I burrow in the tree stump of baser comforts.
Many days not wanting, siphoning desire to avoid residency in my body.
My lipids store his tweaking fat fingers: his controlling interest.
Mind blanks, prostate remembers. You warm me, and *its* prison melts.
Panic birds shriek, protecting memories in the cold room. I keep quilling
and shrinking, months go by, I go on not living well, letting him win.
At times I don't know what *wife* or *husband* mean, I don't know what *I* is.
I love you. You said, "I don't care what you say, just write me real."

Independent Commission for the Location of Victims' Silence

When I was at boarding school in the '80s, you liked to talk
about your brother, the ▮▮▮▮▮ councillor.
And the thought emerges out of marl
like a Tyrannosaur fossil: He knew
the ones who gave the order. Two hundred miles south
of the Belfast Brigade's field
of operations, brindled cows cropping both sides of the Anglo-
Irish avenue, a brook whispering under a low bridge, electric fence
the only filament   I.E.D. glint of a trip wire   In the monastery parlour
you were saying that your mother—"ah, sure God rest her"—had
as an old woman, hosted the Army Council in her living room
and served digestive biscuits.
                              As noduled fingers took the cosy
off the pot, they asked: "So what do you think, Mrs. H.?" Stooped,
she might nod agreement—or, would she suggest juicier targets?
You loved that they loved her for that. Republican Matriarch,
their own personal Mother Ireland.
"Ay, they respected her—and sure, she herself
a little old lady." I imagine her
going back to her rosary in the kitchen, goitred with her sons'
internment, and the long war's soiling.

My father hated the IRA so much
he was almost a Catholic Unionist. I was perverse,
half-proud of your connections—your spadework.
I thought I knew everything about you, Chaplain of the blood
of Pearse, Connolly and Slab Murphy.
But until I was 33, I didn't know you had disappeared me
yourself, into the ground of my body in several monastery rooms
while the whole country was sleeping
                                     and detectives were sent out
in plain clothes and bullet proof in search of the Border Fox
—uzis and handsomeness at check points in West Limerick.

You were a rogue cell, the others nodded as they passed
with their psalters and eyes' *omertà*.
There is no taut white archaeological string to mark
the pit. We know that it happened, and we know that they did it, but
not everyone has been recovered.

Blessing the Blind Man

Inside Reception, where the red clay walls
had an indwelling hush that was Coptic hives
or cool barrel of rain—I was starting
to drink it before you fouled the water—
a blind man on retreat asked: "could I have
your blessing, Father?" "Oh—of *course*!"
you said, unctuous, wearing your monk mask.
Just before, you'd been raging.
Getting on her tour bus, an elderly nun
from the country ventured: "pray for me,
Fr. Narziss?" "*Pray for me, Father?* That fake
fucken piety. *Ara*—don't talk to me!"
Very little chastened you. I said
"I've been learning healing"—was trying
to explain energy, the blind man nodding,
seeming to see, when you cut in, reclaiming
prime orbit: "I respect other traditions, but—
it's just not *Christ*."
                            Watching your hands
an inch above his head, I froze. Maybe
there was a thought, far down—something about
being twenty-two and your paralytic,
still going for healing to the pool that narcotised
me, slipped in a spine, into me—
but if there was, I wouldn't grasp it for 13 years.
Now I am 50, and I am
beside myself. My hands were hot, sublimating
a rage itch. The blind man bowed his head
to receive—so vulnerable, it cuts like a wound.
What did he have that protected him
against your hands? You stood in the silhouette
of the sun: deliberately, haloed. Usurper,
where God should have been.
Even as you blessed, you were aware
of effect and camera angle, like when you said

"if you want to see me as I really am
look at me on the altar on Sunday
as I break the bread." But I have seen you
naked. I've seen you slavering.
So I say: see me stepping, out
of your eclipse, into real sun.

Sandymount Strand, Nocturne

Distant *pee-wit* of waders, winter nights
on the strand for an answer.
The city a shimmer of yellow points,
the tide a mile out, lighthouses sweeping
ahead of you, walking out to sea
clean of the question.

Notes

The Latin proverb is "Qui tacet consentire videtur, ubi loqui debuit ac potuit".

BOOK EPIGRAPH: "In the middle of the road I had a stone / I had a stone in the middle of the road" is from Carlos Drummond de Andrade's original poem in the Portuguese, 'No meio do caminho': "No meio do caminho tinha uma pedra / tinha uma pedra no meio do caminho", translated by Pearse Hutchinson, *Done into English,* Gallery Press, 2003.

BLOCKING: Mariabronn is the fictional monastery in the novel *Narziss and Goldmund,* by Hermann Hesse. (Hesse was educated at Maulbronn Abbey in Germany.)

PILOT FISH: Pilot fish were reputed to lead sharks to food.

CENTRAL PARK, NOCTURNE: The epigraph is from 'City Without Sleep (Nocturne of the Brooklyn Bridge)' ('Ciudad sin sueño', *Poeta en Nueva York*) by Federico García Lorca, translated by Robert Bly in *Selected Poems: Lorca and Jiménez* (Beacon Press, 1973).

THREE PERSON SWORD references a practice whereby Katana swords were tested on "condemned criminals... or their corpses..." p. 55, *Samurai: The Last Warrior,* by John Man (Random House, 2011).

THE ROOM (1998) is for Janne.

STOCKHOLM SYNDROME: the epigraph is from T*he Dictionary of the Irish Language* (Dublin, Royal Irish Academy).

THE ANNALS: "died of hunger at their hands" is from *The Annals of Inisfallen.*

CRONE MOUNTAIN: Cruach Mhárthain is a mountain in West Kerry. The poem's last line is my own translation from Federico García Lorca's 'Romance de la luna, luna': "sus senos de duro estaño."

THE SENIOR FILM: The original Latin for the epigraph is "Quasi modo geniti infantes, rationabile, sine dolo lac concupscite".

TOM CREAN SINGS SEAN-NÓS AT THE TILLER IN THE SOUTHERN OCEAN: "the fourth man" references "third man syndrome", a joint hallucination by Crean, Worsley and Shackleton that there was a fourth man accompanying them as they crossed South Georgia island, close to death. T.S. Eliot altered this to a third man in *The Wasteland*.

CRASH CENTRE: the epigraphs are from *How the Lions Won: The Stories and Skills Behind Two Famous Victories* (edited by Terry O'Connor, Collins, 1975).

HENRY STREET GARDA STATION, REPORTING (2016) is for my mother, Ann McLoghlin (7th April, 1946 – 23rd April, 2022).

Acknowledgements

Grateful acknowledgement is made to the following journals, where some of these poems first appeared, sometimes in a slightly different form: *AMP* (online), *Barrow Street*, *Cimarron Review*, *Copper Nickel*, *Cyphers*, *Éire-Ireland*, *Hayden's Ferry Review*, *Lakeview International Journal of Literature and Arts*, *Map Literary* (online), *Natural Bridge*, *New Madrid*, *New Hibernia Review*, *Poetry Ireland Review*, *Psychology Tomorrow* (online), *Spoon River Poetry Review*, *The Stinging Fly*, *The Stony Thursday Book*.

'Central Park, Nocturne', 'The Drying Room' and 'Porn King' were published in *Open Eyed, Full Throated: An Anthology of American / Irish Poets* (edited by Nathalie Anderson, Arlen House, 2019).

'Crash Centre' was nominated for a Pushcart Prize by the editors of *Natural Bridge* (issue 31, 2014).

'Tom Crean Sings Sean-Nós at the Tiller in the Southern Ocean' was a finalist in the 2015/2016 Ballymaloe International Poetry Prize (now The Moth Poetry Prize), selected by Billy Collins, published in *The Moth*, spring 2016, and *The Sunday Business Post*, 3rd April, 2016.

'Blocking', 'Hostage Walk', 'Bones' Evidence', 'Black Holes', 'Trapped by Trees' were published in the Featured Poet section of *New Hibernia Review*, issue 27:3, autumn 2023.

I would like to thank Jessie Lendennie and Siobhán Hutson of Salmon Poetry, the Munster Literature Centre, the trustees of the Katherine and Patrick Kavanagh Fellowship, as well as Maria Corbett, Carol Coulter, Alex White, One in Four, Patrick Donnelly, Thomas Dooley, Jennifer Horgan, Peter Longofono, Sharon Olds, Patrick Cotter, Richard Prins and Nathan Van Sweden. Thanks to my parents and my family. Most of all, thanks to my wife, Adrienne.

DAVID McLOGHLIN was born in Dublin in 1972, and is a prize-winning poet and writer of creative nonfiction. The author of *Waiting for Saint Brendan and Other Poems* and *Santiago Sketches* (both from Salmon Poetry), his work has appeared widely in literary magazines in the USA and Ireland, and been broadcast on WNYC's *Radiolab*. A Patrick and Katherine Kavanagh Fellowship Recipient in 2023, he was awarded second prize in the Patrick Kavanagh Awards in 2008, was a Teaching Fellow at New York University, won the Open category in the 2018 Voices of War International Poetry Competition and received a major Literature Bursary from The Arts Council in 2006. His writing has been anthologised, most recently in *Distant Summers: Remembering Philip Casey* (Arlen House, 2023) and *Grabbed: Poets and Writers on Sexual Assault, Empowerment & Healing* (Penguin Random House, 2020). He was Resident Writer at Hunts Point Alliance for Children in the South Bronx, and has taught at New York University, University College, Dublin, the American College Dublin, and UCD's innovative Poetry as Commemoration project. He currently facilitates creative writing classes with a variety of organisations, including Poetry Ireland's Writers in Schools and The Center for Fiction (New York). He returned to Ireland in 2020 after 10 years in Brooklyn, NY, and now lives in the Cork area with his wife and daughter.

www.davidmcloghlin.com

Photo copyright Miles Lowry, www.mileslowry.ca

salmonpoetry
Cliffs of Moher, County Clare, Ireland

"Publishing the finest Irish and international literature."
Michael D. Higgins, President of Ireland